Everyday Maths

Ourselves

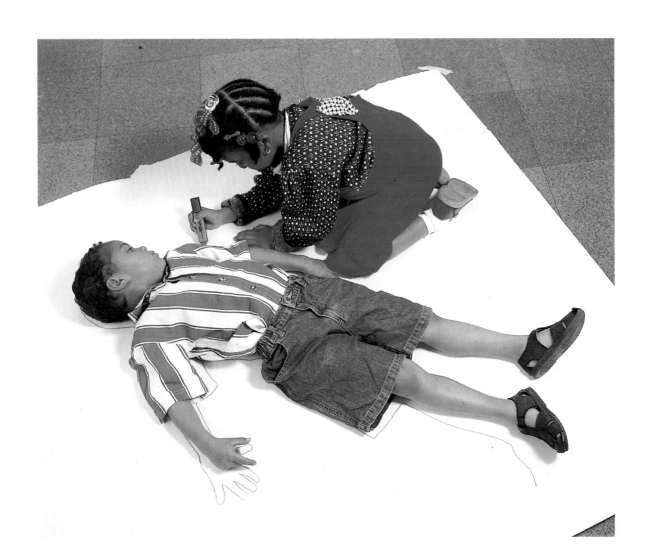

Annie Owen

WAYLAND

Everyday Maths

At Home
Fun with Food
Ourselves
Out and About

First published in 1995 by Wayland (Publishers) Ltd,
61 Western Avenue, Hove, East Sussex BN3 1JD

British Library Cataloguing in Publication Data

Owen, Annie
Ourselves. – (Everyday Maths)
I. Title II. Series
510

ISBN 0-7502-1392-2

Printed and bound in Italy by Rotolito Lombarda, S.p.A., Milan
Design and typesetting by Can Do Design, Buckingham
Illustrations by Clare Mattey

Picture acknowledgements
APM Studios Cover; Brian Armson 5, 8, 10 (three), 15;
Karin Craddock 1, 6, 12, 23; Greg Evans International 22;
Sally and Richard Greenhill 7, 18, 20; Christina Newman 24
(both); Tony Stone Images 14 (both); Wayland 10 (three).

Contents

Words in **bold** in the text are explained in the Glossary on page 28.

 This symbol shows there is an activity to be completed.

Happy Birthday!

Tom and Helen have birthdays today. They are both seven. Tom's birthday cake is in the shape of the number seven. Helen's cake has seven candles on it.

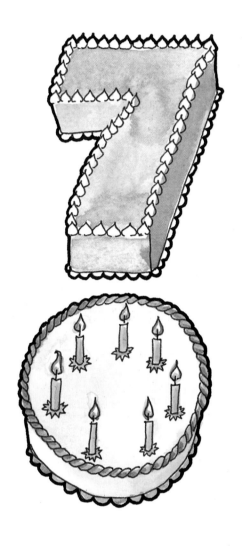

Draw a cake for your own birthday. Make a pattern with the candles.

Now make some different patterns. Here are some patterns with six candles.

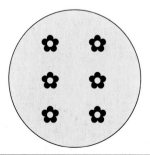 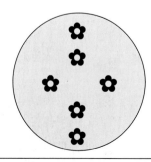 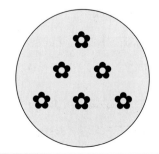

Mark was born on the 16th of April.

April is the fourth month of the year.

The year he was born was 1986.

We write his **date-of-birth** like this:

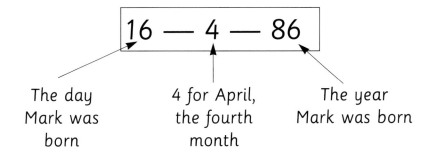

16 — 4 — 86

The day Mark was born | 4 for April, the fourth month | The year Mark was born

We say Mark was born on the
sixteenth of April nineteen eighty-six.

Day — Month — Year

Find out the dates-of-birth of eight people. Write them down in order. Write them like this:

Day – Month – Year

Do any of these people have their birthdays in the same month? Do any of them have their birthdays on the same day and in the same month?

Can you put your own family in order by age?

Body maps

Jane is drawing round David. She is drawing his body map. David can use this to find out his height and his stretch. He uses his **handspans** to measure these. These are handspans.

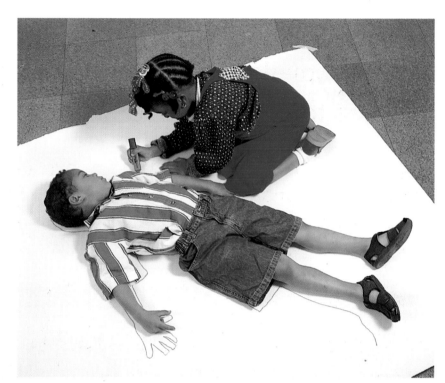

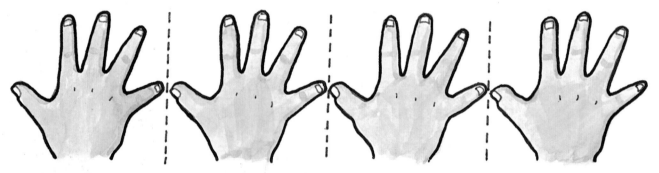

Ask someone to draw around your body. Measure your height and stretch in handspans. Write them down. Help some friends to do the same and look at the measurements. What do you notice?

Think of some other measures you could use to do this. You could use the length of your foot.

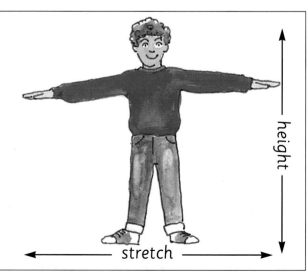

Sometimes we need to measure things
which are too small for handspans.
Sometimes we can use string to
measure smaller things. We use a tape
measure to get very close answers.

Choose two friends. Use string
to measure round the head, waist
and wrist of each friend. Ask them
to measure your head, waist and
wrist with string. Which measure is
the biggest? Use a tape measure to
find out who has the smallest and
the biggest waist measure.

Our pets

Many families keep animals as pets.

Ask ten children about the pets in their families. Make a **tally chart** like this:

Which is the most popular pet?

Dog	////
Cat	//// /
Hamster	/
Goldfish	//

Find out the colour of each pet. Record your answers on a **bar chart** like this:

What colour are most of the pets?

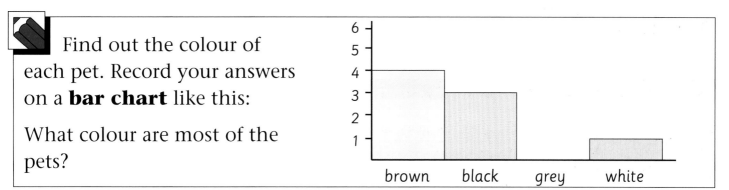

We look after our pets to keep them fit and well. Leroy helps to look after the class hamster. Here is the diary he has written for one day.

School starts. Hammy is running on his wheel.

Lucy and James fill the food tray and change the water.

I give Hammy a piece of carrot.

Hammy hides because we make too much noise.

I say goodbye to Hammy.
He is asleep.

Pairs

A pair means two. You have a pair of eyes. You have a pair of hands.

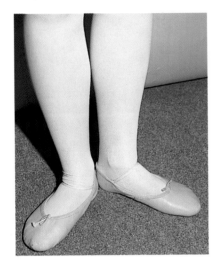

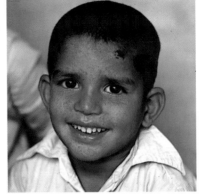

You have a pair of feet. Socks come in pairs as well. If you have 1 pair of socks, you have 2 socks. Write a table like this:

1 pair	=	2 socks
2 pairs	=	4 socks
3 pairs	=	
4 pairs	=	
5 pairs	=	

What do you add each time?

These numbers

    2   4   6   8   10

are called **even numbers**.

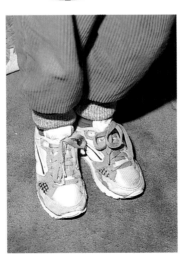

If you had 5 socks that were the same how many pairs could you make? Would there be any socks left over? Write your answer like this:

5 socks = 2 pairs + 1 left over

Find some other numbers which leave one over when you have made a pair.

These numbers are called **odd numbers**.

1 3 5 7 9

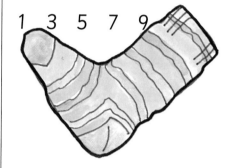

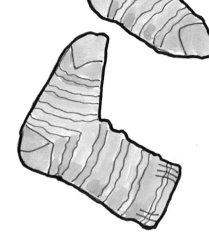

Write each number from 1 to 20 on a small piece of paper. Make two piles like this:

Put the even numbers in one pile and the odd numbers in the other pile.

Even

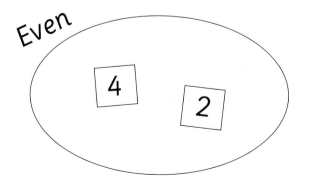

4 2

Odd

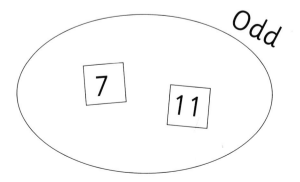

7 11

Pocket money

Some parents give their children pocket money.

Jacinta gets £1 pocket money each week. This is what she does with her money:

Comics — 50p

Sweets — 30p

Save — 20p

———

£1.00

If you had £1 pocket money each week, what would you do with it? Make a list like Jacinta.

Choose something that you would like to save up for. Write down how much it costs. If you saved 10p a week, how long would it take for you to have enough money to buy it? Use a calculator to help you do this.

When you save money you need a place to keep it. Many children put their savings into a money box.

You can make your own money box. You will need some card and a square to draw round. Draw a shape like this:

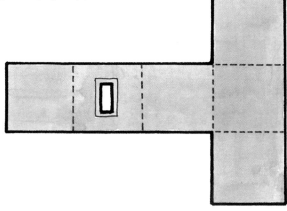

This shape is called a **net**. Ask an adult to cut a slit in one side. Draw tabs like this so you can stick your box together.

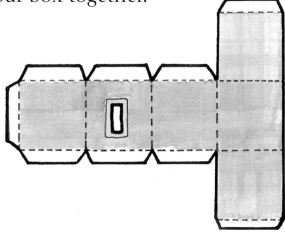

Cut a slit in one side to let the money in.

Ask an adult to help you cut out your net. Fold the tabs and stick your box together. Now you can paint your money box if you wish.

The best time of day

Jay thinks early morning is the best time of day. Ben thinks the evening is best. Leroy likes the afternoon most.

▼ Leroy likes half past four in the afternoon the best, when his big brother takes him swimming.

Make a chart like this to show the best times of day for each person. Now make a chart for yourself and your friends.

	morning	afternoon	evening
Jay			
Ben			
Leroy			

► The best time for Jay is after breakfast at 8 o'clock in the morning.

These clocks show the times that each person likes best. Write down the times shown on each clock. There are two ways to do this. Draw your own clock to show the best time of day for you.

Jay

Ben

Leroy

▶ Ben likes the evening the best. Then he can read on his own. We can also write 7 o'clock in the evening as 7pm. Morning times are am.

Use numbers only to write down the times that Ben likes best. There are two different ways to do this.

The clean and tidy game

You will need:

1 die with faces 2,2,4,4,6,6

1 counter for each player

How to play:

1. Place all the counters outside the bath, near the duck.

2. Take turns to throw the die.

3. Move your counter the number of squares shown on the die. You move in the direction of the numbers.

4. If you land on a square where there is a job to be done, you miss a turn. Keeping clean and tidy takes time!

5. If you land on the plug-hole you must go back to the start.

6. The first person to land on the 40 square is the winner.

Dressing up

We often change the clothes we wear. Clothes for bed are different from clothes for school.

We also wear different clothes when the weather changes. Summer clothes keep us cool and winter clothes keep us warm.

These pictures are muddled up.

The squares to make the summer picture are B4, A3, C2 and D1. Write them in a list. Now make lists of the squares for the winter picture, the bedtime picture and the school picture.

Clothes are made from material. The material may be one colour or it may have a pattern with different colours.

Harry is going to make a pattern for his material. He starts with a shape like this:

Here are some of the patterns he can make.

This pattern **repeats** along a straight line.

This pattern reflects sideways.

This pattern reflects downwards.

This pattern makes a quarter turn each time it is repeated.

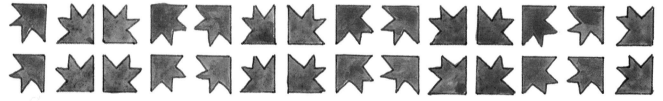

Make your own pattern. Draw a shape. Choose one of the ways to make a pattern. Use your shape to make the pattern.

Off to school

No two schools are the same. Children learn about different things at different times. In some countries children only go to school in the mornings. Some children also go to school on Saturdays.

This is David's school timetable.

What does David do on Friday at 11 o'clock? What does he do on Wednesday afternoon?

Make a timetable of a week in your class.

	Mon	Tue	Wed	Thur	Fri
9.00 - 10.15 a.m.	Reading	Reading	Maths	Reading	Maths
PLAY					
10.45 a.m.- 12.15 p.m.	History	Maths	Geography	Maths	Maths
LUNCH					
1.15 - 3.00 p.m.	Art	History	P.E.	Geography	Music

Some children walk to school. Other children go to school on a bus. Can you think of some other ways children get to school?

Find out how 12 children in your class get to school. Record the answers in a **pictogram** like this:

Show your pictogram to some adults. Ask them if children got to school in the same ways when they were children. What was different?

Keeping fit

We all need exercise to keep fit and well. Sometimes your heart and muscles need to work hard to stay strong and healthy. Your body needs exercise to keep it moving properly.

You can count your heart-beats if you put a finger (not a thumb) on the inside of your wrist.

Ask an adult to time 10 seconds with a stop-watch while you count your heartbeats. Then try these exercises. Count your heartbeats for 10 seconds after each one. Write the results in a table like this:

	Heartbeat in 10 sec
No exercise	
Walk quickly around hall	
Run quickly around hall	
Jump up and down ten times	

We need to practise our sports to play them better. Try to do each of the things on this chart three times. Ask a friend to help you time each one. Record your results each time.

Stretching

How many times can you stretch your hands above your head in one minute?

Ball skills

How many times can you bounce a football in one minute?

Jumps

How many star jumps can you do in one minute?

Our families

Some families are big and some families are small.

▶ Here are Toby's family:

They are standing in order of age. Toby is older than the dog. How much older is Toby than the dog?

Mum	Dad	Toby	Poppy	Gwilym
24.12.56	01.07.57	24.12.82	01.05.85	10.08.87

▶ Toby's family are now standing in order of height.

Write down the names of everyone in your family. Put them in order of age. Find other ways to put them in order. Make up some questions to ask about them.

The people in a family can be put on a 'family tree' to see how they are related. Here are Li Ling's and Martin's family trees:

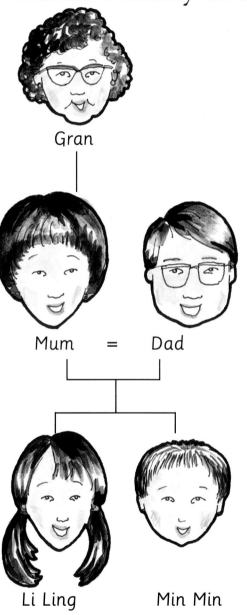

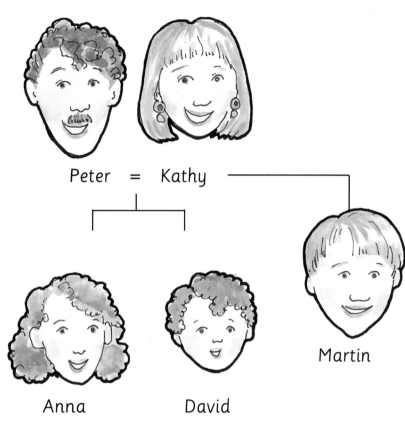

Draw your family's tree. You can add people who do not live with you and people who have died if you like.

Someone special

Everyone is different. We may think
that some things about us are special.
Other people may think that different
things about us are special.

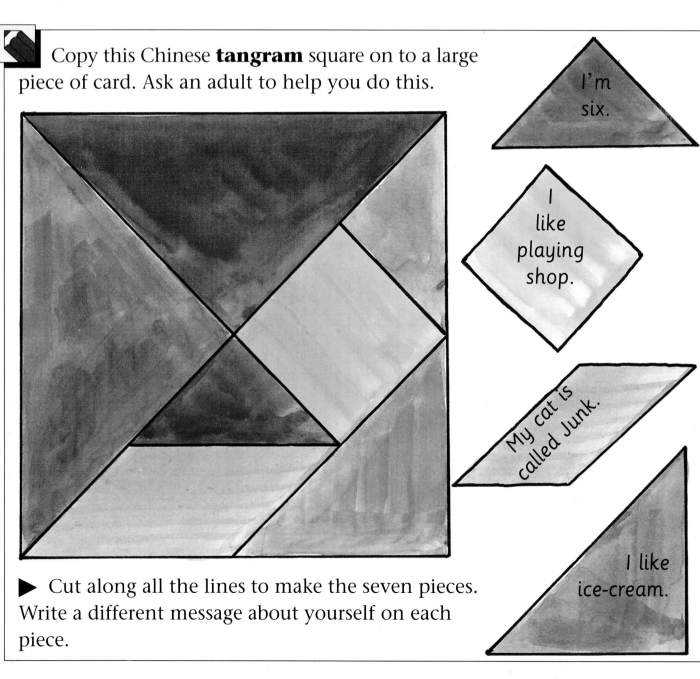

Copy this Chinese **tangram** square on to a large
piece of card. Ask an adult to help you do this.

I'm six.

I like playing shop.

My cat is called Junk.

I like ice-cream.

▶ Cut along all the lines to make the seven pieces.
Write a different message about yourself on each
piece.

Make a picture with your tangram pieces. Stick the pieces on to a large piece of paper. Then you will have a picture about someone special – you.

People have played with Chinese tangrams for hundreds of years. They can be made into lots of different pictures.

Make some more tangrams. See how many different pictures you can make. Here are some ideas.

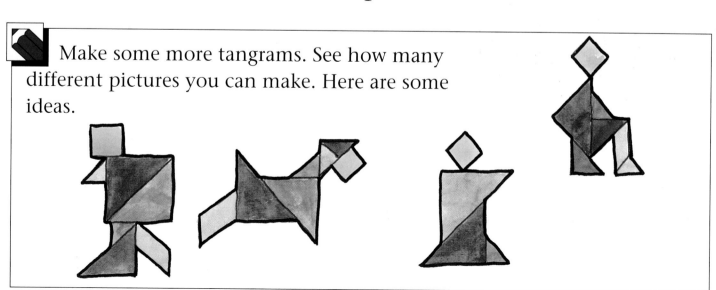

Glossary

Date-of-birth
A date of birth is written like this: day-month-year. So 7-10-89 means that the person was born on the 7th day of October, 1989.

$$7{-}10{-}89$$

Day   Month   Year

Even numbers
These are whole numbers which can be divided by two.

$$2 \div 2 = 1 \qquad 6 \div 2 = 3$$
$$4 \div 2 = 2 \qquad 8 \div 2 = 4$$

Handspan
A handspan is the width of the biggest stretch you can make with one hand. You can use your handspan to measure the lengths of different things.

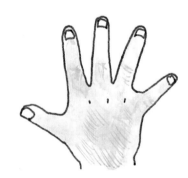

Net
A net is a flat shape which can be folded up to make a solid shape. You need tabs and glue to hold the net together when you make a solid shape.

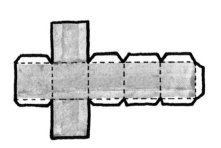

Odd numbers
These are whole numbers which cannot be divided by two.

3   5   7   9

Pictogram

This a picture which gives you information without using words. Pictograms are often used in places such as airports where people may not read English.

Reflect

When you look at things in a mirror they look flipped over. This is called a reflection. The mirror reflects things.

Rotate

When you turn things round, but don't move them along, you rotate them. The hands of a clock rotate.

Tally chart

A way of recording the amounts which are being counted in groups of five. One line or mark is made for each item. The first four items are marked with straight lines. The fifth item is marked with a line that goes across the four straight lines.

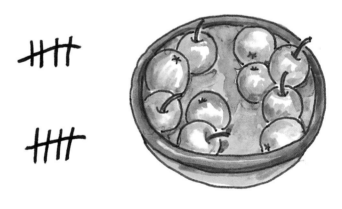

Tangram

A tangram is a Chinese puzzle which is made from pieces of card. The pieces can always be put together to make a square. You can make pictures by putting the pieces together in different ways.

Notes for parents and teachers

Page 4/5

Many children find chronology difficult to understand. Talking about birthdays and comparing the ages of friends, younger brothers or sisters will help to reinforce this concept. Encourage children to talk about the passing of time and the different ways in which we record time – in days, months and years.

Children could experiment with the patterns they make using numbers to 10.

Page 6/7

The stretch of a person is usually very close to their height.

Children should have plenty of opportunities to make direct comparisons between objects which are longer, taller, thicker etc., before they start to use non-standard measures such as handspans to measure length. They will need to have lots of practice using non-standard measures before they are introduced to standard units of measurement, and start using rulers and tape measures.

Page 8/9

When younger children begin to use tally charts straight lines are enough. However, it is important to introduce the 'five-barred gate' method – four straight marks with the fifth going across, to help them count their items more quickly. Children should also become aware of some of the different ways of handling data and recording it. A comparison could be made between bar and tally charts to do this.

Before children write their own day diaries for a pet, make sure that they understand how to tell and record the time using clock faces and the 'hands' of the clock. The meaning and use of am and pm should be explained.

Page 10/11

Odd and even numbers are the first categories of numbers that children encounter. Take every opportunity to discuss them. For example, house numbers on streets where the odd numbers are on one side and the even numbers on the other side. This is a good way of introducing or reinforcing the concept of odd and even numbers.

Give children the opportunity to discuss the different 'pairs' they can name for parts of the body – such as hands, feet, ears etc. They may not realize that nostrils and thumbs are also 'pairs'.

Page 12/13

Children may need guidance from an adult when they choose an item to save for. You may wish to introduce a limit – not more than £2 for example, so that they can calculate the rate of saving more easily.

A net is a flat (2D) shape which when folded makes a solid (3D) shape. The six squares have to be arranged so that they make a cube when they are folded. Not all arrangements of the squares will make a cube.

Children could investigate how some boxes e.g. those used for cereals, are stuck together, before they start work on their own boxes. They could then discuss where the tabs should go, so that the net for their cubes can be stuck together more easily.

Page 14/15

This is a good opportunity to reinforce the everyday language concerning time and gives good practice in using the 12-hour analogue clock. Children should understand these concepts very well before they are asked to undertake the more advanced activities.

Page 16/17

The game reinforces number and counting in an enjoyable way. Make sure that the children understand the rules before they start to play. They could be asked to think of variations which would speed up the game – e.g. throw again when they land on the plug-hole, rather than starting again.

Page 18/19

The body puzzle introduces children to the concept of co-ordinates. Young children find the usual notation (number/number) confusing. Number/letter co-ordinates provides an easier introduction to this concept.

There are many examples of different kinds of patterns in the natural and home environments. Children could be asked to observe different patterns and discuss how they are made. The examples cover repeating, reflecting and rotational patterns. You may wish to extend activities to discuss reflection and rotation in more depth.

Page 20/21

A pictogram is one of the simplest types of information display. Each item of information has its own picture, rather than a square on a bar chart. One difficulty for young children is that they do not draw all their pictures the same size and then are mislead by information on the chart. To help them, you could either give them squares of paper to draw on, or squared paper so that each item is drawn to the same size within the square.

Page 22/23

If you have access to a simple timing device such as a rotoscan, children can time each other when they do these activities. Otherwise an adult will need to do the timing, while another child can do the counting.

These activities are not competitive. Should you wish to use competitive sports, tables of individual or class performance could be compiled, and discussion could then take place about the fastest, longest, highest or most accurate scores/achievements.

Measurement of length can be in standard or non-standard units, depending on the stage each child has reached in understanding and using these measures.

Page 24/25

You may wish to introduce the concept of order using 1st, 2nd and 3rd. Children could then discuss the many different ways in which things can be ordered – such as height, weight, units of time etc.

There is also the opportunity to discuss distance – how far away different members of a family live from their 'home' town. The time it takes to travel to see them using different methods of transport could also be discussed.

The family tree activity gives the opportunity for children to handle data, think logically and present the information accordingly.

Page 26/27

The Chinese tangram puzzle is an ancient puzzle from which hundreds of pictures can be made. The mathematical value of the puzzle lies in recognizing the properties of the shapes; the introduction of right angles and 'half' right angles; the conservation of area (although the pictures may look larger then the original square, they are made from the same amount of card).

A note about computers

If you have access to a simple data base with graph facilities, then you can use any of the data collection activities in this book as an opportunity to introduce children to such software. Pie charts can then be introduced in place of bar charts on occasions. Young children cannot draw pie charts, but they can recognize the relative sizes of the sections.

Index

B

bar chart   9

C

clocks   9, 15

E

even numbers   10, 11

M

measuring   6, 7
money   12, 13

O

odd numbers   11

P

patterns   4, 19

S

shapes   13, 19, 26, 27

T

tally chart   8
time   9, 14, 15, 22, 23
timetable   20